VIETNAM

Vietnam

Jen Green

Peter Zinoman and Hy V. Luong, Consultants

NATIONAL GEOGRAPHIC

WASHINGTON, D.C.

Contents

Foreword

To many people in the West, the word "Vietnam" suggests the image of a war-ravaged and poor country. Vietnam has undoubtedly been war-ravaged, as two generations of Vietnamese successively fought French, American, and Chinese forces on its soil from 1946 to 1979. Vietnam has also been poor. However, modern Vietnam is much more than a war-torn country. It is a society with over 80 million people, with thousands of years of history, a rich environment that is home to many rare species of plants and animals, a long and beautiful coastline, diverse cultural traditions among its various ethnic groups, and quite a few UNESCO-designated World Heritage sites, ranging from the natural beauty of Ha Long Bay to cultural sites at Hue and My Son. Vietnam has also made enormous economic strides in the past two decades. It has become a leading world exporter of rice, coffee, pepper, and cashews, among other agricultural products. It has also annually exported billions of dollars in manufactured goods such as garments, footwear, and electronics. Thanks to this strong economic growth, more than one third of all Vietnamese have escaped poverty in the past fifteen years. Whereas 20 years ago, Hanoi and Ho Chi Minh City, the two biggest cities in Vietnam, had mainly bicycles in the streets, today a growing number of urban households in the upper middle class own cars. In 2007, about one fifth of all Vietnamese were estimated to have access to the Internet. At the same time, Vietnam faces many challenges: congested cities, increasing environmental pollution, and growing urban-rural inequality, among others.

This book for elementary school students has succeeded in presenting in a simple writing style basic information about Vietnam. It writes about Vietnam not as a war episode in French or U.S. history, but as a society with a long history, rich cultural traditions, and a dynamic economy.

▲ Flower vendors
wearing traditional
conical hats crowd
the streets with their
bicycles.

Hy V. Luong

Hy V. Luong
University of Toronto

Mountains
and
Coast

THE VIETNAMESE SAY THAT THEIR country is shaped like a long pole bending under the strain of two heavy rice baskets at each end. Vietnam is one of the narrowest countries in the world, about 1,025 miles (1,640 km) long from north to south, and just 30 miles (48 km) wide at its narrowest point. The entire eastern side of the country is a long coastline bustling with fishing boats and barges in many places. Most of the inland area is steep mountain ranges. Only in the north and south are there large areas of flat land. These are the rice baskets—the areas of farmland where most food is grown. Each year, heavy monsoon rains fall over the mountains and lowlands. Streams tumble downhill to flood the rice fields, or paddies, on the plains.

◄ Vietnamese boats, known as *sampans*, travel along the Perfume River in central Vietnam. The river flows from the mountains in the west to the ocean in the east.

HOT AND WET

Vietnam has a tropical climate. It is generally hot for most of the year. However, the country's long shape means that the weather in the north is often very different from the conditions in the south. The far north of Vietnam is hot in summer. In winter, icy winds blow south from China and temperatures may fall to near freezing. Cool, drizzly rain falls for several days on end in spring. In the south, conditions are hotter and wetter. Most of the rain falls in summer and fall. The mountains of central Vietnam are cooler and generally drier than the coastal lowlands. In summer, hurricanes, known as typhoons in the Pacific, hit the long coast. Labels on this map and on similar maps throughout this book identify most of the places pictured in each chapter.

Fast Facts

OFFICIAL NAME: Socialist Republic of Vietnam

FORM OF GOVERNMENT: Socialist republic

CAPITAL: Hanoi

POPULATION: 84,402,966

OFFICIAL LANGUAGE: Vietnamese

CURRENCY: dong

AREA: 127,123 square miles (329,247 square kilometers)

BORDERING NATIONS: Cambodia, Laos, China

HIGHEST POINT: Fan Si Pan, 10,315 feet (3,144 meters)

LOWEST POINT: Sea level, 0 feet (0 meters)

MAJOR MOUNTAIN RANGES: Truong Son range (also called Annam Cordillera)

MAJOR RIVERS: Mekong, Red, Ma, Perfume

Average Temperature & Rainfall

Average High/Low Temperatures; Yearly Rainfall

HANOI (NORTH):
82°F (28°C) / 68°F (20°C); 66 in (168 cm)

DA NANG (CENTRAL):
84°F (29°C) / 72°F (22°C); 74 in (188 cm)

HO CHI MINH CITY (SOUTH):
90°F (32°C) / 73°F (23°C); 78 in (198 cm)

South China Sea

MAP KEY
Mild
Humid subtropical
Tropical
Tropical wet
Tropical wet and dry

0   mi   200
0   km   200

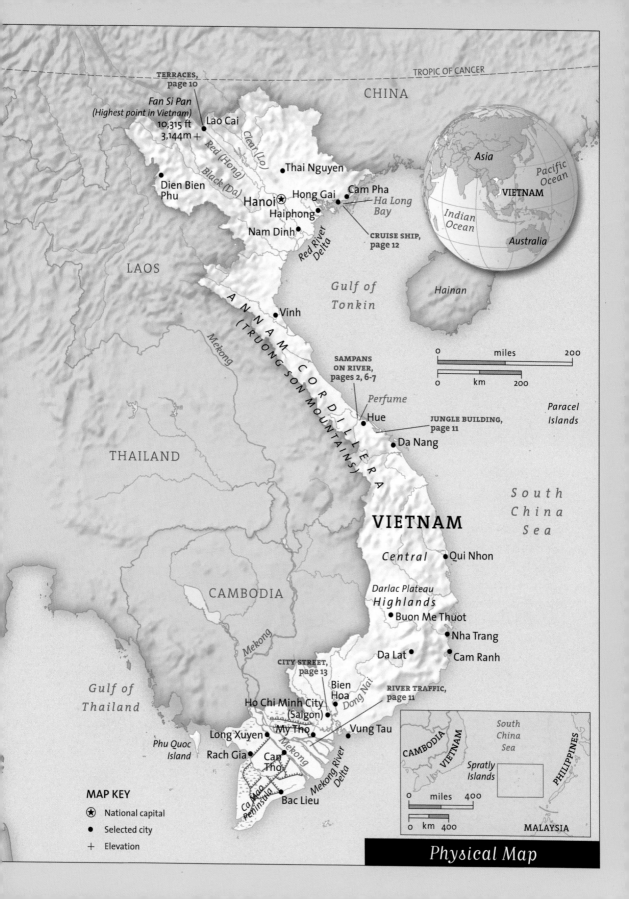

CHINA

TERRACES,
page 10

Fan Si Pan
(Highest point in Vietnam)
10,315 ft
3,144m ✛ ● Lao Cai

Clear (Lo)

Red (Hong)

Black (Da)

● Thai Nguyen

Dien Bien
Phu ●

Hanoi ✪   ● Hong Gai ● Cam Pha
  Haiphong ●   Ha Long
              Bay

Nam Dinh ●

Red River
Delta

CRUISE SHIP,
page 12

LAOS

A N N A M   C O R D I L L E R A
(TRUONG SON MOUNTAINS)

● Vinh

Gulf of
Tonkin

Hainan

Asia   Pacific
                  Ocean
        VIETNAM
Indian
Ocean

          Australia

0   miles   200

0   km   200

Paracel
Islands

Mekong

SAMPANS
ON RIVER,
pages 2, 6-7

Perfume

Hue ●

JUNGLE BUILDING,
page 11

● Da Nang

THAILAND

South
China
Sea

VIETNAM

Central   ● Qui Nhon

Darlac Plateau
Highlands

CAMBODIA

● Buon Me Thuot

Mekong

● Nha Trang
Da Lat ●   ● Cam Ranh

CITY STREET,
page 13

Bien
Hoa ●

Dong Nai

RIVER TRAFFIC,
page 11

Ho Chi Minh City
(Saigon) ●

My Tho ●

Gulf of
Thailand

Long Xuyen ●

Phu Quoc
Island

Rach Gia ●

Mekong

Can
Tho ●

● Vung Tau

CAMBODIA   VIETNAM   South
                     China
                     Sea

Spratly
Islands

PHILIPPINES

0   miles   400

0   km   400

MALAYSIA

Ca Mau
Peninsula

● Bac Lieu

Mekong River
Delta

MAP KEY

✪ National capital

● Selected city

✛ Elevation

Physical Map

Coastal Country

Vietnam lies in Southeast Asia, on the eastern edge of
the bulging peninsula known as Indochina. China is
Vietnam's mighty neighbor to the north, Laos and
Cambodia are to the west. In the east, Vietnam's
coastline is washed by the South China Sea. Long and
thin, Vietnam is shaped like a slender letter S. It has
about the same area as the U.S. state of New Mexico.

The country's two "rice baskets"—the fertile plains
to the north and south—are fed by two of Asia's
greatest rivers, the Red and Mekong. They collect
water from the mountains far inside Vietnam's
neighboring countries. Once the rivers arrive on

RIVER OF THE NINE DRAGONS

The Mekong River is the third-largest river in Asia, after China's Yangtze and the Ganges in India. Every second, the Mekong dumps enough water into the sea to fill 44,000 Olympic-sized swimming pools. It would take the river just over 12 hours to fill Lake Erie. The river rises in Tibet and flows for 2,600 miles (4,180 km) through Myanmar, Laos, Thailand, and Cambodia before reaching Vietnam's southern coast.

The Vietnamese name, River of the Nine Dragons, refers to the way the Mekong splits into nine branches as it weaves towards the sea. Over millions of years, mud from the river water has built up to form a huge area of swamp known as the Mekong Delta. The highest point in the delta is just 9 feet (3 m). The Mekong Delta is one of Vietnam's main rice-growing areas.

▶ The many channels of the Mekong Delta are always busy with boat traffic.

Vietnam's plains, they contain immense amounts of silty water. Both rivers split into several channels before they reach the sea. In the Mekong Delta, river water sometimes floods out of the channels. Its silt settles to the ground, covering the plains with a layer of fertile mud.

Mountain Chain

Three-quarters of Vietnam is covered by mountains. The main range is the Truong Son Mountains that run down the west of the country. In the

▼ An imperial tomb stands on a wooded hill near Hue. Vietnam's hills were once covered in forest, but many areas have now been cleared.

HILLS IN THE SEA

Ha Long Bay, east of Hanoi, has some of the finest coastal scenery found anywhere in the world. Along a 75-mile (120-km) stretch beside the Gulf of Tonkin, some 2,000 rounded towers of limestone rise from the sea. Sheer cliffs and weird rock formations loom out of the mist as cruise boats slowly move among the islands. There are numerous caves and grottos with spectacular stalagmites and stalactites. The bay's name means "descending dragon." Legend has it the islands were created when a giant dragon rushed down to the sea to defend the land from invasion. In its haste, it gouged deep trenches and threw up rocky peaks with its huge feet and swishing tail.

▲ A cruise ship approaches the limestone islands of Ha Long Bay.

narrow central region, the mountain peaks form the western border with Laos and Cambodia. The mountains drop steeply eastward to the ocean. In some places mountain spurs reach the coast and form rugged cliffs that plunge into the sea. However, most of the coast has a narrow strip of flat land that is used for farming. Crops are also grown on high plateaus between mountain peaks. The steep hillsides are cut into little steps to create more flat land where crops can be grown.

From High to Low

The highest peak in the country is Fan Si Pan. It is located in the northwest, where Vietnam's mountains meet the Yunnan Mountains of southern China. The Red River flows past Fan Si Pan, before it is met by several other mountain rivers, including the Black and Clear Rivers.

Lowlands cover only a quarter of the country. The Red River creates a muddy plain in the north, but the largest low-lying area is the immense Mekong Delta in the south. It is the only part of the country that is not fringed by mountains.

WHOSE ISLANDS ARE THEY?

In the South China Sea, midway between Vietnam and the Philippines are the Spratly Islands. Vietnam claims these tiny coral islands as its own. However, China, Malaysia, Taiwan, Brunei, and the Philippines also lay claim to them. The islands are too small to live on, but the seabed nearby is thought to contain reserves of natural gas and oil, which makes the Spratlys very valuable. Vietnam once planned to send tourists to the islands to try to improve its claim to the land—but no one wanted to go.

▲ A lighthouse stands on An Bang, one of the largest of the Spratlys. Vietnam and other nations maintain small military forces on different islands.

Crowded Cities

Vietnam's two largest cities are located in the flatlands of the deltas. In the north, the capital, Hanoi, lies on the Red River. A city of many lakes and waterways, it has a population of 2 million. Far to the south is Ho Chi Minh City, formerly called Saigon. Vietnam's largest city, with 5.1 million people, this thriving port is the country's main center for trade and business.

▼ Bicycles and scooters stream along a busy street in Ho Chi Minh City.

With such a long coast, it is no surprise that Vietnam's other major cities are by the sea. These include the important port cities of Haiphong and Da Nang.

Hidden Wonders

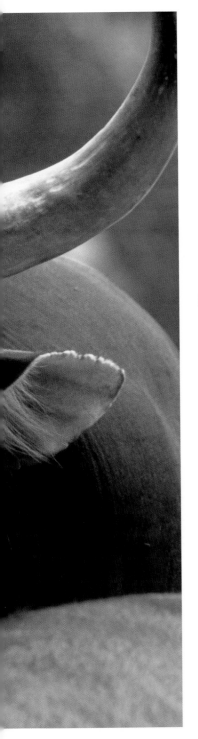

THE FORESTS OF VIETNAM have kept many secrets over the years. The country's rugged landscape is difficult to explore, and many jungle species have remained undiscovered until recently. In 1937, scientists came across a type of wild ox called the kouprey, for the first time. Today, koupreys are still very rare. Herds of other forest cattle, such as gaurs and bantengs, are more common.

In 1994, scientists discovered another amazing animal in Vietnam. The saola is a goat-sized relative of cattle and antelopes. It has a brown coat with white stripes and curved horns. Local people call saolas "polite animals" because they move quietly through the forest. The shy saola is a symbol of all of Vietnam's wildlife—rare and in need of protection.

◀ The banteng is a wild ox that lives in the forests of Vietnam and across Southeast Asia. It is a close relative of the domestic cattle that are farmed around the world.

VARIED HABITATS

Vietnam's mountainous terrain, wetlands, and long coastline contain many different habitats. Grasslands, caves, steep rocky cliffs, and several types of forests make up the land. Water habitats include rivers, lakes, and swamps, with coral reefs offshore. The map opposite shows the main vegetation zones—what plants grow where in Vietnam. Each zone is home to a distinct group of plants and animals.

Over 270 types of mammals, 180 reptiles, and 80 amphibians have been identified in Vietnam. There are 800 bird species, including hornbills and pheasants. Many of the rare animals are protected by law, but poaching is a problem. Across Vietnam, 30 national parks and reserves have been set up to protect natural habitats.

▶ Douc langurs are brightly colored. They have maroon legs and reddish patches around the eyes. Their colors allow the monkeys to see each other through the trees.

Species at Risk

Vietnam's forested hills and swampy jungles are home to many rare and unusual animals. However, much of the country's delicate forest habitats has been cleared to make way for coffee and tea plantations. The patches of forests that remain are often barely large enough for some animals to survive in them. Other forests are also regularly damaged by people cutting firewood or logging trees for lumber. This makes it difficult for wildlife communities to thrive. Chemicals dropped by U.S. aircraft during the Vietnam War have also harmed large areas of forest.

Species at risk include:
> Douc langur (monkey)
> Giant catfish
> Indochinese tiger
> Kouprey (cattle)
> Saola (antelope)
> Sumatran rhino
> Tonkin snub-nosed monkey

TROPIC OF CANCER

CHINA

CHINA

*Muong Cha
Nature Reserve*

Ba Be N.P.

**MONKEY,
page 16**

MYANMAR

Clear (Lo)

Red (Hong)

Black (Da)

Tam Dao N.P.

Hanoi ⊛

*Ha Long
Bay*

LAOS

*Ba Vi
N.P.*

Haiphong •

*Cat Ba
N.P.*

*Cuc Phuong
N.P.*

*Red River
Delta*

*Gulf of
Tonkin*

Hainan

*Pu Luong
Nature Reserve*

Pu Mat N.P.

*Vu Quang
N.P.*

Ke Go Nature Reserve

Phong Nha-Ke Bang N.P.

A N N A M   C O R D I L L E R A

(TRUONG SON MOUNTAINS)

Mekong

THAILAND

*Bach Ma
N.P.*

*South
China
Sea*

Central

**WILD OX,
pages 2, 14-15
AND
TIGER,
page 18
AND
TAPIR,
page 19
AND
DHOLE,
page 20**

Darlac Plateau

CAMBODIA

Highlands

*Yok Don
N.P.*

Mekong

*Cat Tien
N.P.*

Dong Nai

**BOAT IN SWAMP,
page 20**

*Gulf of
Thailand*

*Tram Chim
N.P.*

Ho Chi Minh City
(Saigon) •

*Phuc Quoc
N.P.*

Mekong

**MUDSKIPPERS,
page 21**

*U Minh
N.P.*

*Mekong River
Delta*

MAP KEY

Primary vegetation zones/ecosystems

- Mangroves
- Tropical and subtropical dry broadleaf forests
- Tropical and subtropical moist broadleaf forests

Protected Lands

- Selected national parks and nature reserves

*Mui Ca Mau
N.P.*

*Con Dao
N.P.*

| 0 | miles | 200 |

| 0 | km | 200 |

Vegetation & Ecosystems Map

▲ Vietnam produces a lot of inexpensive wood—some of it is stolen from protected forests.

▼ An Indochinese tiger crosses a forest stream. Unlike most other cats, tigers often take a swim.

Precious Forests

A few hundred years ago, tropical forests covered most of Vietnam and much of the rest of Southeast Asia. Now many of the trees that grew in the valleys and on the lowlands have been replaced by fields with rice paddies and plantations for growing tea, coffee, rubber, and sugarcane.

Upland regions that are too steep for fields are still covered by forests. At the highest levels, where the forests are usually cloaked in mist, moss covers the trees. Montane forests, which contain shorter trees than lowland forests, grow on lower slopes. In many areas, logging and forest clearance

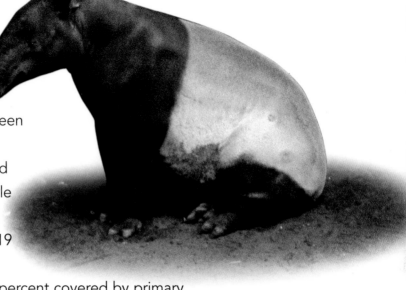

has left only small patches of broadleaf forest.

Ancient rain forest that has never been disturbed by loggers or woodcutters is called primary forest. Very little of Vietnam's primary forest remains. Today 19 percent of the land is forested, with only 10 percent covered by primary forest. The government has launched a replanting program, but the forests that grow back will never be as rich in wildlife as the ones that were there before.

▲ Tapirs are strange-looking relatives of rhinos and horses. These rare animals live in Vietnam's forests.

Jungle Living

Vietnam's forests contain at least 12,000 species of plants, probably many more. They include mighty trees, with pillar-like roots, and delicate flowers such as orchids. Forest mammals include boars, oxen, and deer, which are hunted by wild dogs called dholes, and big cats such as leopards and tigers. Black bears and elephants also roam remote forests.

Less familiar animals, such as tough-skinned Asian rhinos and shy

SPRAYING THE FOREST

During the Vietnam War, U.S. aircraft sprayed Agent Orange, a mixture of strong weedkillers, on Vietnamese forests. The aim was to kill trees, which concealed enemy soldiers and also provided them with food. Nineteen million gallons (72 million liters) of chemicals were sprayed by planes, helicopters, and tanks, destroying not only forests but also fields and orchards. An explosive liquid called napalm was also used to burn the trees. Some areas of the countryside have still to recover because the chemicals remain in the environment. They cause serious health problems for both people and wildlife. Many areas are now covered with thick weeds known as American grass, which grow in place of the trees.

RED DOGS

The dhole, or Asian red dog, is a dog like no other. It does not bark, but lets out scary whistles and screams. Dholes live in the dense mountain forests of Vietnam. These wild dogs live in packs of between 5 and 12 animals. They always hunt together, fanning out through the forests to flush out prey hiding in the undergrowth. A pack of dholes can tackle prey, such as deer or ox, which are much larger than a single dog. However, unlike other pack animals, dholes do not share their food. Instead each dog eats as fast as possible, to make sure it gets enough to eat. Dholes sometimes begin to feed before their prey has died.

▲ Dholes have short and wide muzzles, which gives them a stronger bite than wolves or any other wild dog.

tapirs also live in the forests. Tapirs use their long, flexible noses to root out fruits and buds to eat. The tapir's rounded body is white, while its head and legs are black. This coloring breaks up its outline, which makes it hard to see among the trees.

In the Mud

Vietnam's freshwater wetlands include rivers, lakes, and ponds. Wildlife also thrives in canals and drainage ditches. River estuaries, coastal deltas, and many stretches of shore are covered by mangrove forests. The roots and lower trunks of mangrove trees are covered by salty water twice a day, as tides rise and fall. When the water goes down, the knobby, stilt-like roots stick out of the mud. The U-Minh region in the Mekong Delta

▼ Woodcutters travel through the U-Minh mangrove swamp in southern Vietnam to collect firewood.

covers 386 square miles (1,000 sq km)—it is one of the world's largest mangrove swamps.

Poisonous chemicals dropped during the Vietnam War harmed this environment, but the vegetation is now recovering. Vietnam's wetlands are home to over 80 species of frog and salamander, rare crocodiles and turtles, and many waterbirds. Hundreds of different fish include the bizarre mudskipper, which scurries over the mud of swamps on its fleshy fins.

Out to Sea

Parts of Vietnam's coasts and its islands are fringed by coral reefs. These delicate reefs are made by relatives of jellyfish that have thin chalky skeletons. The corals thrive in warm, clear, shallow water and grow on rocky surfaces. When corals die, their skeletons form a thin, hard layer. New corals grow on top, and over millions of years the layers build up into massive reefs full of life and color. More than 1,000 species of fish live around the reefs and coast.

Out at sea, thousands of islands contain some species found nowhere else. Half of the large Cat Ba Island in Ha Long Bay is a wildlife sanctuary. Its forests, lakes, and swamps contain wild boar, deer, monkeys, porcupines, and spectacular birdlife.

▲ Mudskippers are fish that climb out of the water onto mudflats to eat insects. They do not breathe air like we do. Instead, oxygen passes into their blood through their damp skin.

A
History
of
Struggle

FOR MANY PEOPLE, the U.S.-led war of the 1960s and '70s is the first thing that comes to mind when hearing about Vietnam. But over the past 1,000 years, many wars have raged in Vietnam—against China, France, and Japan—as the country fought to be an independent nation.

It all began in A.D. 939, at the Bach Dang River near the modern port of Haiphong. It was there that General Ngo Quyen defeated the Chinese navy. Vietnam had not long been independent; the victory confirmed its independence. Ngo Quyen sunk the Chinese invasion fleet using iron-tipped stakes hidden below the surface of the river. The great victory made Ngo Quyen a national hero, but it was just the beginning of Vietnam's struggle for nationhood.

◀ Vietnam was at war for much of the second half of the 20th century. Evidence of fighting scarred the country, like this downed U.S. bomber in a Hanoi suburb.

CHANGING RULERS

Much of Vietnam's history is divided into dynasties—periods during which members of one family ruled the country. After the Ngo kings took the throne, Vietnam became a place of relative peace and prosperity. Arts and the economy thrived, and the kingdom gradually increased its territory. However, the calm periods were sometimes shattered by bursts of violence as rival families fought for control.

Vietnam's last dynasty, the Nguyen, ruled from 1802 to 1945. For some of this time, the Nguyens ruled in name only, and Vietnam was a colony of France. The French divided Vietnam into three regions: Tonkin in the north, Annam in the center, and Cochinchina in the south. In 1954, the French were driven out, and Vietnam was divided into two countries. This situation led to the Vietnam War (1960–75), when Vietnam was the focus of a conflict between communists and U.S.-led forces. In 1975 Vietnam was finally united under communist rule.

▲ **A woman visits the tomb of Tu Duc, the last king of Vietnam before France took over in 1884.**

Time line

This chart shows the approximate dates for some of the ruling dynasties and other periods in the history of Vietnam. Between 1954 and 1975 the country was split into North Vietnam and South Vietnam.

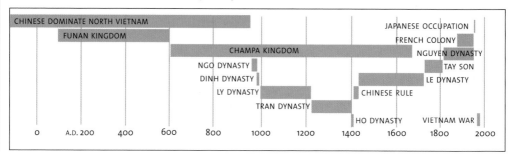

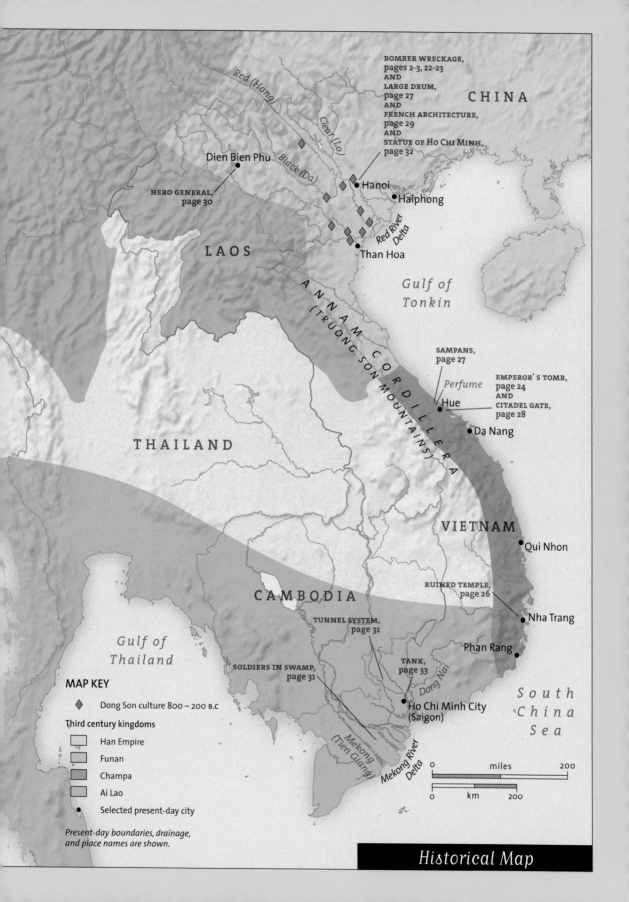

BOMBER WRECKAGE,
pages 2-3, 22-23
AND
LARGE DRUM,
page 27
AND
FRENCH ARCHITECTURE,
page 29
AND
STATUE OF HO CHI MINH,
page 32

CHINA

Red (Hong)

Clear (Lo)

Black (Da)

Dien Bien Phu

HERO GENERAL,
page 30

LAOS

Hanoi

Haiphong

Red River
Delta

Than Hoa

Gulf of
Tonkin

SAMPANS,
page 27

Perfume

EMPEROR'S TOMB,
page 24
AND
CITADEL GATE,
page 28

Hue

Da Nang

A N N A M C O R D I L L E R A
(TRUONG SON MOUNTAINS)

THAILAND

VIETNAM

Qui Nhon

RUINED TEMPLE,
page 26

CAMBODIA

Nha Trang

TUNNEL SYSTEM,
page 31

Phan Rang

Dong Nai

Gulf of
Thailand

SOLDIERS IN SWAMP,
page 31

TANK,
page 33

South
China
Sea

Ho Chi Minh City
(Saigon)

Mekong
(Tien Giang)

Mekong River
Delta

MAP KEY

◆   Dong Son culture 800 – 200 B.C

Third century kingdoms

☐   Han Empire

☐   Funan

☐   Champa

☐   Ai Lao

●   Selected present-day city

*Present-day boundaries, drainage,
and place names are shown.*

miles   0   200

km   0   200

Historical Map

An Ancient Past

Vietnam's first civilization began about 5,000 years ago in the Red River Valley in the north. These first Vietnamese knew how to grow rice and make tools and weapons out of bronze. Until the 3rd century B.C., a civilization flourished in the northern region, which was ruled by a family called the Hungs. In 207 B.C. a Chinese lord, Trieu Da, conquered the north and established a kingdom called Nam Viet.

▲ The Po Nagar towers in Nha Trang are the remains of a Hindu temple built during the Champa Kingdom in the 7th century A.D.

Three Kingdoms

In 111 B.C., Nam Viet became part of the Chinese empire. China controlled north Vietnam for the next 1,000 years. Nam Viet's people kept their own language, but were influenced by the Chinese in other ways. For example, they learned Chinese farming skills, such as plowing and irrigation. The Chinese also brought new religions to the region: Confucianism, Taoism, and Buddhism.

While China ruled the north, two other kingdoms flourished in south and central Vietnam. A Cham kingdom developed in central Vietnam beginning in the 2nd century A.D. around the sea port of Da Nang. The Chams built tower-like temples. This civilization

had links with India to the west, and its people were Hindus.

Another Hindu kingdom, Funan, developed in the Mekong Delta. The south of Vietnam was later conquered by the Khmer people from neighboring Cambodia before joining Vietnam, largely in the 1700s.

Becoming One

In A.D. 939, Ngo Quyen drove away the Chinese. His dynasty—the Ngo (the family name comes first in Vietnam)—was later replaced by others. In 1054, the first Ly king renamed his land Dai Viet. Despite the changes, the region was a place of peace and learning. Vietnam's first university, the Temple of Literature in Hanoi, was founded in 1070. Meanwhile Dai Viet gradually extended its territory south.

In 1407, the Chinese took control once more. But in 1428 Vietnamese general Le Loi drove them out. The Le dynasty continued Dai Viet's expansion, gradually taking territory from Champa.

By the mid-1500s, two families, the Trinh and the Nguyen, had set up rival

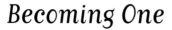
▲ Covered sampans are rowed along the Perfume River as they have been for thousands of years.

▼ A bronze drum used in Confucian ceremonies is housed in a pagoda at Hanoi's Temple of Literature.

BESIDE THE PERFUME RIVER

Hue on the Perfume River in central Vietnam is one of the nation's most historic cities. In the 16th century it became the home of the Nguyen family, and in 1802, Prince Nguyen Anh made it the capital of Vietnam. The Nguyen emperors built a beautiful Imperial Citadel with temples and gardens on the north bank of the river. The Citadel is surrounded by a high wall that is 7 miles (11 km) long. At its heart is the Forbidden Purple City, where the emperors lived—ordinary people were not allowed in. During the Vietnam War, the Citadel was badly damaged, but parts have since been rebuilt.

▶ The Noon Gate, the main entrance into the Imperial Citadel in Hue, is kept spotlessly clean.

kingdoms—the Trinh in the north, and the Nguyen in the south. The rivalry led to a 45-year civil war that ended in a stalemate, but in 1771 three brothers led a revolt called the Tay Son Rebellion. They temporarily took control of Dai Viet.

While Vietnam was divided, Europeans began to arrive, mainly missionaries and traders from Portugal and later France. In 1784, the last Nguyen lord, Nguyen Anh, asked the French to help him defeat the rebels. The lord became victorious in 1802 and ruled over a reunited country, which he renamed Vietnam.

A French Colony

Beginning in the 1860s, the French began to take over Vietnam. First they took the south, which they called Cochinchina, then Annam in the center, and Tonkin in the north. By the 1890s the French controlled the eastern part of Southeast Asia forming a territory named Indochina.

The French improved ports and built roads and railways to transport Vietnam's natural resources. The colonial rulers also improved education and medicine for all, but apart from a few landowners, most Vietnamese gained little else. Meanwhile French colonists became very wealthy and lived in luxury. They set up large plantations to grow rubber, coffee, and tea. The land of many highland communities was taken away and turned into plantations.

▲ Older buildings in Vietnam's cities were influenced by French architecture.

▼ Ho Chi Minh led Vietnam's communist independence movement.

Communist Rebels

Resistance to French rule grew steadily. By the 20th centuty, the most powerful rebels were the Vietnamese Communist Party, which was led by Ho Chi Minh.

In 1939, the outbreak of World War II shifted the power balance in Southeast

A BRILLIANT GENERAL

Vo Nguyen Giap is the greatest general in Vietnam's recent history. Before his military career he was a history teacher. He then joined the Communist Party and became a close advisor to Ho Chi Minh. During the 1940s, Giap trained soldiers to launch surprise attacks on Japanese forces rather than fight in major battles.

General Giap is known for two great military victories. The first was in 1954 when he masterminded victory over the French at Dien Bien Phu. He continued to command the communist forces after the French left, and in 1968, he helped launch the Tet Offensive. This operation involved troops attacking hundreds of U.S. bases at once. The American forces fought back well, but the increase in violence turned the U.S. public against the war and paved the way for a communist victory in 1975. General Giap served as Minister of Defense in the new government until 1980.

◀ General Vo Nguyen Giap greets villagers at Dien Bien Phu in 1994 where his soldiers defeated French troops 40 years before. That battle ended French rule in Vietnam.

Asia. The Germans occupied France and that allowed Germany's ally, Japan, to take control of Vietnam from the French. In response, Ho Chi Minh launched the Viet Minh—an organization dedicated to fight for an independent Vietnam.

In August 1945, World War II ended with Japan's surrender. The Vietnamese communists lost no time in proclaiming themselves as an independent nation— the Democratic Republic of Vietnam (DRV). Ho Chi Minh hoped that the United States would support the new country. However, the U.S. government feared the spread of communism in Asia. The Americans did not want Vietnam to become a new ally of the Soviet Union—an enemy communist empire centered in Russia.

Freedom Fighters

After World War II, the French tried to take back their colonies in Indochina, including Vietnam. They set up the Associated State of Vietnam (ASV). This led to the Indochina War between France and the Viet Minh.

The United States supported France, while the Soviet Union and China supported the Viet Minh, who were strong in the north and center. In 1954 the Viet Minh defeated the French at the Battle of Dien Bien Phu.

▲ Vietnamese soldiers make their way through the swamps of the Mekong Delta. Wars raged across Vietnam almost constantly from 1945 to 1975.

AN UNDERGROUND CITY

Today Cu Chi is a suburb of Ho Chi Minh City—formerly called Saigon, but now renamed after the communist leader. During the Vietnam War, Cu Chi was the site of an underground military fortress used by communist forces. Its network of tunnels had a hospital, classrooms, and bomb factories, and part of it lay directly under a U.S. base! From the heart of enemy territory, 125 miles (200 km) of tunnels led right to the Cambodian border. The tunnels were used to launch raids against South Vietnamese and U.S. forces. The U.S. military eventually discovered the tunnel network, but never managed to destroy it completely. Parts of the network can now be viewed by tourists, but most of it remains untouched since the end of the war.

▲ A tour guide emerges from the Cu Chi tunnels through a hidden trapdoor.

Following this victory, France, the United States, the Soviet Union, China, and representatives of the DRV and ASV met in Switzerland to negotiate peace terms. They temporarily divided Vietnam into two countries: communist North Vietnam and non-communist South Vietnam. The country was meant to be reunified following national elections, but they were never held.

The Vietnam War

In 1957, communist rebels in the south rose up against South Vietnam's government. The rebels, called the Viet Cong, were supported by Ho Chi Minh's North Vietnam. They were supplied with weapons from the north by sea and via the jungles of Laos and Cambodia. Later North Vietnam's army also joined the fighting.

▼ A giant statue of Ho Chi Minh, the founding father of modern Vietnam, looms above Vietnamese people in Hanoi.

Other countries soon became involved. The Soviet Union and China supported the north, while South Vietnam was backed by the United States. By the late-1960s half a million U.S. troops were in Vietnam fighting the communists. U.S. planes bombed North Vietnam's cities and the Viet Cong's supply lines in Laos and Cambodia. They also dropped millions of

THE BOAT PEOPLE

▲ About 2,500 boat people crowd onto a single ship in 1978.

After the communist victory in 1975, one million South Vietnamese fled the country on boats. These refugees became known as the boat people. Many boats sank in treacherous waters or were raided by pirates. Refugees who made it to a safe country were often told to leave again. The lucky ones were allowed to stay in Hong Kong, Malaysia, Thailand, Indonesia, and the Philippines, where they were housed in camps set up by the United Nations. Many refugees were resettled in the United States, Canada, Australia, or France. In the mid-1990s the camps were closed, and the last refugees were sent back to Vietnam.

gallons of Agent Orange, poisonous chemicals that destroyed the forests believed to hide the enemy. But they failed to reduce the support for Ho Chi Minh.

The U.S. public became unhappy with their soldiers fighting in a foreign country. In 1973, a ceasefire allowed U.S. troops to withdraw from Vietnam, but the fighting was not over. Two years later, the communists overran the south and took its capital, Saigon. After an election, a communist government created a single country—the Socialist Republic of Vietnam.

▼ North Vietnamese troops roll into Saigon on a tank at the end of the Vietnam War in 1975.

Among
the
Pagodas

ON EVERY DAY OF THE YEAR, you'll find a festival going on somewhere in Vietnam. Religious holidays and the changing seasons are observed along with celebrations of political events and important military victories. Wrestling matches, singing contests, and buffalo fights may be part of the fun. There are also dragon dances, with several people hidden inside a long, spectacular costume dancing to the beat of gongs, cymbals, and drums.

Tet, the largest festival in Vietnam, celebrates the New Year—according to the phases of the moon—with fireworks and feasting (noisy firecrackers were recently banned). Vietnam's festivals are a showcase of its rich culture and varied customs.

◀ Colorful lanterns are on sale in Cholon, a business district in Ho Chi Minh City. The Vietnamese buy lanterns for the Moon Festival in the fall.

A GROWING POPULATION

Vietnam has a population of about 85 million, more than any other country on the Southeast Asian mainland. However, the population is not evenly spread throughout the land. Three-quarters of Vietnamese live in the lowlands, especially in the Red and Mekong River basins.

About 86 percent of the population are Kinh, or ethnic Vietnamese. The other 14 percent is made up of 53 different groups such as the Hmong, Dao, Muong and Khmer, who mostly live in mountain areas. There are also Chinese people, known as the Hoa, most of whom live in cities.

▶ A Dao girl visits a market in a hill town in northwest Vietnam.

Common Vietnamese Phrases

Vietnam's official language is Vietnamese. The mountain peoples have their own languages. In ancient times Vietnamese was influenced by Chinese. The language was first written down using Chinese characters. In the early 1900s, the Vietnamese began to use the Roman alphabet—the one used by English speakers. Vietnamese is very difficult to speak because words have different meanings depending on how high- or low-pitched your voice is.

Hello / Goodbye	Chao (chow)
Please	Lam on (lam uhn)
Thank you	Cam on (kam uhn)
Yes	Co (cuhr)
No	Khong (kuhng)
My name is	Ten cua toi la (tehn coya toy lah)
Excuse me	Xin loi (sin luhy)

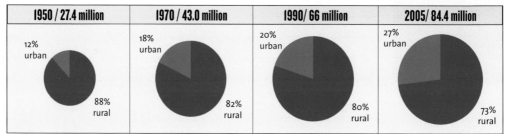

1950 / 27.4 million	1970 / 43.0 million	1990 / 66 million	2005 / 84.4 million
12% urban / 88% rural	18% urban / 82% rural	20% urban / 80% rural	27% urban / 73% rural

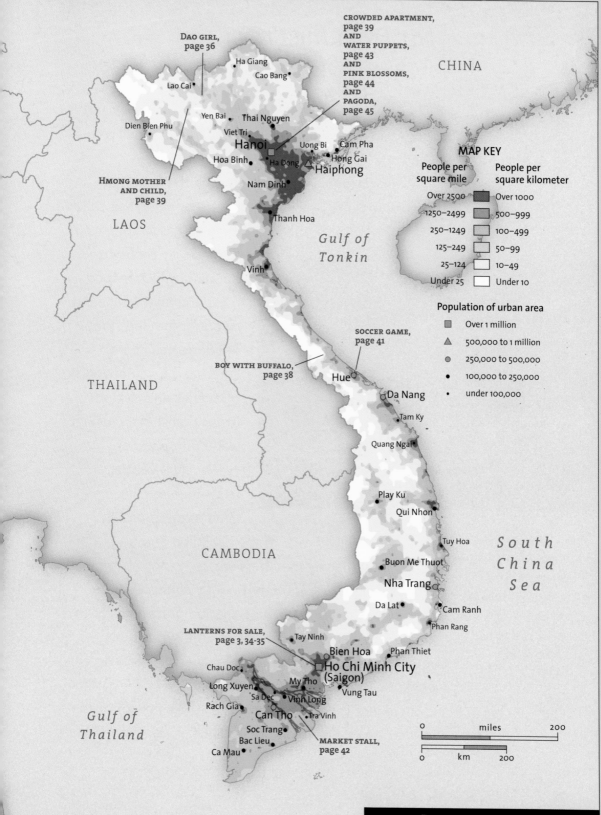

CHINA

DAO GIRL,
page 36

Ha Giang

Cao Bang

Lao Cai

CROWDED APARTMENT,
page 39
AND
WATER PUPPETS,
page 43
AND
PINK BLOSSOMS,
page 44
AND
PAGODA,
page 45

Yen Bai

Thai Nguyen

Dien Bien Phu

Viet Tri

Hanoi

Uong Bi

Cam Pha

Hoa Binh

Ha Dong

Hong Gai

Haiphong

HMONG MOTHER
AND CHILD,
page 39

Nam Dinh

LAOS

Thanh Hoa

*Gulf of
Tonkin*

Vinh

MAP KEY

People per
square mile

People per
square kilometer

Over 2500   Over 1000

1250–2499   500–999

250–1249   100–499

125–249   50–99

25–124   10–49

Under 25   Under 10

Population of urban area

⬜ Over 1 million

△ 500,000 to 1 million

⬤ 250,000 to 500,000

• 100,000 to 250,000

· under 100,000

SOCCER GAME,
page 41

BOY WITH BUFFALO,
page 38

THAILAND

Hue

Da Nang

Tam Ky

Quang Ngai

Play Ku

Qui Nhon

CAMBODIA

Tuy Hoa

*South
China
Sea*

Buon Me Thuot

Nha Trang

Da Lat

Cam Ranh

Phan Rang

LANTERNS FOR SALE,
page 3, 34-35

Tay Ninh

Bien Hoa

Phan Thiet

Chau Doc

Ho Chi Minh City
(Saigon)

Long Xuyen

My Tho

Sa Dec

Vinh Long

Vung Tau

Rach Gia

Can Tho

Tra Vinh

*Gulf of
Thailand*

Soc Trang

Bac Lieu

MARKET STALL,
page 42

Ca Mau

0   miles   200

0   km   200

Population Map

Far From the Crowds

Three-quarters of Vietnam's population lives in the countryside. Many country-dwellers are farmers, growing crops such as rice. Farmers use tractors and other farm machines; but water buffalo still pull plows and carts in places.

Most communities are located in the flat delta regions of north and south Vietnam or along the coast. These areas were traditionally prone to flooding, which helped make the land fertile and good for farming. Today, the floodwaters are controlled by a network of ditches and dykes (small dams) that channel water into paddies.

Family is central to Vietnamese life. Grandparents usually share a house with one of their children and his or her family. Other family members set up homes elsewhere. Women in the country wear brightly colored blouses over loose trousers and cone-shaped grass hats called *non la*. The hats shade them from the sun and also keep the rain off their heads. Men wear shirts and trousers. They rarely wear traditional non la.

In recent years, many country people have moved to the cities to find work. Cities such as Hanoi and Ho

▲ A boy rides a water buffalo past rice paddies in central Vietnam. Although rice farms do use machinery, the rice plants are usually planted by hand.

Chi Minh City have become very crowded and noisy with traffic. Many city-dwellers find work in factories. In cities you might see women wearing the traditional outfit, the *ao dai*, a high-collared shirt worn over wide trousers. Dresses and skirts are more common nowadays, but the ao dai is still worn at celebrations such as weddings. City men wear thin shirts and trousers.

▲ Space is tight in Vietnam's cities. This large Hanoi family sleeps and eats in a tiny room.

School Days

In Vietnam people believe education is very important. When the communist government took power, schooling became a top priority. Education standards

THE HIGHLANDERS

Vietnam's mountains are home to several hill peoples, whose beliefs, customs, and languages are different from those of most Vietnamese. They include the Muong, Dao, and Hmong people of the northern mountains, and the Ede and Giarai of uplands farther south. Such groups are called *Montagnards*, a French term meaning "highlanders." Many of the groups are related to people from nearby nations, such as Thailand, Laos, and Cambodia. Montagnards are mainly farmers, and some are nomadic, clearing a patch of forest to grow crops for a few years before moving on. Their unusual life styles and a strong community spirit have ensured highland traditions survive.

▲ A Hmong child is carried through the mountain drizzle by its mother.

are high, and nine out of ten people over the age of 15 can read and write.

All children between the ages of 6 and 15 must go to school. Only the first five years of schooling are free. With only a few years in which to learn what they need, Vietnamese students have to work very hard. Children go to school six days a week, with many pupils having private lessons on Sundays. After five years parents must pay a small fee to educate their children. A few children from the very poorest families leave school before the age of fifteen and begin to work in the fields or as street vendors.

NATIONAL HOLIDAYS

The Vietnamese have many festivals throughout the year, in addition to holidays. People do not have time off for festivals marked with an asterisk:

▲ Young men rest in the shade during the celebrations for Youth Day, held each March.

JANUARY 1	New Year's Day
LATE JANUARY/ EARLY FEBRUARY	Tet
FEBRUARY 3	Anniversary of the founding of the Vietnamese Communist Party*
MARCH 8	Women's Day*
MARCH 26	Youth Day*
APRIL 30	Saigon Liberation Day
MAY 1	International Labor Day
MAY 19	Ho Chi Minh's birthday*
JUNE 1	Children's Day*
JULY 27	Memorial Day*
AUGUST 19	Anniversary of the August 1945 Revolution*
SEPTEMBER 2	National Day
NOVEMBER 20	Teachers' Day*
DECEMBER 22	Army Day*

Spare Time

Whatever their age, the people of Vietnam work long hours especially during harvest time. On their days off, people play soccer, table tennis, and volleyball. With so much water nearby, some Vietnamese also go swimming. Many people practice Vietnamese martial arts, such as *vovinam*, as well as martial arts introduced from other countries, like kung fu, judo, and tae kwon do. During festivals, chess games are staged using people in costumes as chess pieces. People also relax at home by listening to the radio or watching television—if they have one. Even in cities, nearly 10 percent of people do not own a TV; in rural areas, the number is even higher.

▲ Schoolchildren march in a parade on Children's Day in June.

▼ Boys play soccer outside the walls of the Imperial Citadel in Hue.

What's Cooking?

Vietnamese food is a tasty blend of Thai and Chinese cooking styles. Many dishes make use of locally caught fish or shellfish, and an abundance of homegrown fruits and vegetables. The staple food is rice, either boiled, fried, or made into

HOT SOUP

▲ A tasty bowl of *pho bo*—beef and noodle soup.

Vietnam's national dish is *pho*—noodle soup, served steaming hot. The long noodles are cooked in a broth with chicken, beef, and other ingredients. Each region produces its own version of pho, and some are very spicy! Traditionally pho—pronounced "fuhr"—is prepared by simmering the broth overnight, without allowing it to boil. The dish is relatively new and became popular in the 1950s. Some experts claim it is a mixture of French and Asian cuisine—a French broth mixed with Asian noodles and spices. Many Vietnamese city dwellers eat it daily, often for breakfast or a late snack. The soup is not as popular in the countryside.

▼ A trader takes a rest while at a market in the Mekong Delta.

noodles, and served with vegetables, tofu (bean curd), seafood, egg, or meat. Noodle soup is very popular, as are spring rolls—fried rolls of thin rice paper stuffed with vegetables and meat. A tangy fish sauce called *nuoc mam* is sprinkled on almost everything. In cities, bakeries produce fresh baguettes—French loaves—like those made in the days when the country was ruled by France. The most popular drinks are tea, *nuoc chanh*—fresh lemonade, and soda.

Drama With a Difference

Storytelling and music have been important for centuries. Water puppet shows are unique to Vietnam. Brightly painted wooden puppets perform on a stage provided by a water surface—traditionally the village fish pond. The puppets are worked by puppeteers standing waist-deep in water, using long bamboo poles. Shows are performed at night so the puppeteers remain hidden in the dark. The puppets themselves are lit by floating lanterns.

Puppet shows and dramas acted by human players are accompanied by music from traditional instruments such as flutes, lutes, and xylophones. Traditional folk theater, called *cheo*, and most popular in the north, features three main characters: the hero, heroine, and a clown. Court theater is more formal, with epic tales performed by actors in elaborate makeup.

▼ Vibrantly painted puppets poke above the surface of a pool during a Vietnamese puppet show.

Three in One

As a country governed by communists, Vietnam has no official religion. However, people are allowed to worship if they want. Many Vietnamese follow the "Three Teachings" that came originally from China. They are Confucianism, Taoism, and Buddhism. Confucianism stems from the writings of the Chinese philosopher Confucius, who stressed the importance of duty and respect for one's elders. Followers honor the spirits of their ancestors at little shrines at home. Taoism encourages living in harmony with nature. Buddhists follow the teachings of a Nepalese prince. He believed that leading a pure life would end a person's suffering.

Some of the Vietnamese, especially the highland peoples, practice Animism, the worship of natural forces. There are also Christians, mainly Roman Catholics, and a small number of Muslims.

Festival Time

The Vietnamese worship at pagodas—temples, with one or two tiers of curving roofs. People pray at pagodas and burn incense as an offering to the gods.

Festivals dot the Vietnamese calendar. Dragonboat races are held in midsummer. At the full-moon festival in September, children parade with lanterns and eat fruit cakes.

Tet is the main festival of the year. Celebrations last for a week. Tet celebrates the start of a new year and begins at the last new moon before the spring planting season. People decorate their homes with sprays of peach blossoms, once thought to ward off evil spirits. In the run-up to Tet, people visit family graves and make offerings to their ancestors. Families also exchange presents and visit their local pagoda.

▲ Buddhist monks and nuns file past a shrine. Vietnamese follow two types of Buddhism—one arrived from India, the other came from China.

ONE PILLAR PAGODA

One of the most visited temples in Vietnam is Hanoi's One Pillar Pagoda. This small wooden temple (*right*) stands atop a single pillar in a pool. The shape represents a lotus flower rising from muddy waters—a Buddhist symbol of purity. The original temple is said to have been built in A.D. 1049 by Emperor Ly Thai To, a lonely ruler who had no heir. According to legend, the emperor dreamed that the goddess of mercy appeared to him seated on a lotus flower, holding out a baby boy. Soon after, the emperor married a peasant girl who bore an heir. He thanked the goddess by building the pagoda. The temple has been rebuilt several times, including after retreating French troops destroyed it in 1954.

A New Direction

HANOI MAY BE VIETNAM'S CAPITAL CITY, but Ho Chi Minh City is the business center of the nation. The city, which was known as Saigon until 1975, is young by Vietnamese standards: It is only 300 years old. The city was redeveloped when the French arrived in Vietnam. The French built wide, tree-lined avenues, improved the docks on the Saigon River, and made the city a railroad hub.

Now the modern city is changing again. Gleaming office buildings rise above the winding streets of the old quarter. Internet cafés and shopping malls are replacing rundown markets. Businesspeople stand on street corners, making deals on their mobile phones. The city's commercial spirit is sweeping the nation as an alternative to old-style communism.

◀ The streets of Ho Chi Minh City are busy with traffic most of the time. Heavy traffic is one unwanted product of economic success.

PROVINCES OF VIETNAM

Vietnam is divided into 59 provinces called *tinh*. In addition, there are five municipalities —large cities with the status of a province: Hanoi, Ho Chi Minh City, Haiphong, Da Nang, and Can Tho. Every province and municipality has a People's Council elected by the public. The councils in turn elect a People's Committee, which govern the regions. The central government groups the provinces into eight regions: the northwest, northeast, Red River Delta, Central Highlands, north-central coast, south-central coast, southeast, and Mekong River Delta.

▶ Workers at a factory in the extreme south of Vietnam peel the shells from shrimp before they are packaged and flown to markets across the world.

Trading Partners

Between 1975 and the late 1980s, Vietnam's main trading partners were other communist countries, especially the Soviet Union. After the collapse of the Soviet Union in the 1990s, trade with other Asian countries became more important. Trade with the United States and Europe is also increasing. Vietnam exports crude oil, seafood, rice, shoes, rubber, electronics, coffee, and clothing. It imports machinery, petroleum products, wheat, and cement.

Country	Percent Vietnam exports
United States	18.3%
Japan	13.6%,
China	9.0%,
Australia	7.9%
Singapore	5.6%
All others combined	45.6%

Country	Percent Vietnam imports
China	15.6%
Singapore	12.4%
Taiwan	11.7%
Japan	11.1%
South Korea	9.7%
Thailand	6.5%
All others combined	33.0%

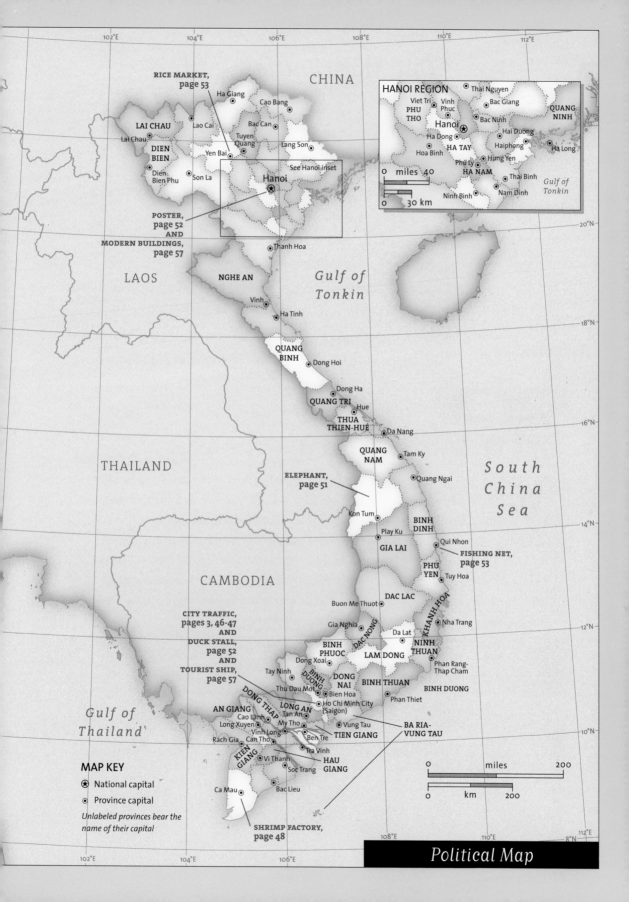

CHINA

RICE MARKET,
page 53

Ha Giang

Cao Bang

LAI CHAU

Lao Cai

Bac Can

Lai Chau

Tuyen
Quang

Lang Son

DIEN
BIEN

Yen Bai

Dien
Bien Phu

Son La

Hanoi

See Hanoi inset

POSTER,
page 52
AND
MODERN BUILDINGS,
page 57

LAOS

Thanh Hoa

NGHE AN

Gulf of
Tonkin

Vinh

Ha Tinh

QUANG
BINH

Dong Hoi

Dong Ha

QUANG TRI

Hue

THUA
THIEN-HUÉ

Da Nang

THAILAND

QUANG
NAM

Tam Ky

Quang Ngai

South
China
Sea

ELEPHANT,
page 51

Kon Tum

BINH
DINH

Play Ku

Qui Nhon

GIA LAI

FISHING NET,
page 53

PHU
YEN

Tuy Hoa

CAMBODIA

DAC LAC

Buon Me Thuot

CITY TRAFFIC,
pages 3, 46-47
AND
DUCK STALL,
page 52
AND
TOURIST SHIP,
page 57

Gia Nghia

DAC NONG

Da Lat

KHANH HOA

Nha Trang

BINH
PHUOC

LAM DONG

NINH
THUAN

Dong Xoai

Tay Ninh

BINH
DUONG

DONG
NAI

BINH THUAN

Phan Rang-
Thap Cham

Thu Dau Mot

Bien Hoa

BINH DUONG

Gulf of
Thailand

DONG THAP

AN GIANG

LONG AN

Ho Chi Minh City
(Saigon)

Phan Thiet

Cao Lanh

Tan An

Long Xuyen

My Tho

Rach Gia

Vinh Long

Can Tho

Ben Tre

Vung Tau

TIEN GIANG

BA RIA-
VUNG TAU

Tra Vinh

KIEN
GIANG

Vi Thanh

HAU
GIANG

Soc Trang

Ca Mau

Bac Lieu

MAP KEY

⊛ National capital

◉ Province capital

*Unlabeled provinces bear the
name of their capital*

SHRIMP FACTORY,
page 48

HANOI REGION

Thai Nguyen

Viet Tri

Vinh
Phuc

Bac Giang

PHU
THO

Bac Ninh

QUANG
NINH

Hanoi

Ha Dong

Hai Duong

HA TAY

Haiphong

Ha Long

Hoa Binh

Phu Ly

Hung Yen

HA NAM

Thai Binh

Gulf of
Tonkin

miles 40

Ninh Binh

Nam Dinh

30 km

Political Map

One More Battle

In 1975, Vietnam's communist government ruled a country completely devastated by war. Over 1.7 million Vietnamese had died in the conflict. A few cities, such as Hue, lay in ruins. Much of the countryside contained hidden landmines, and roads, railroads, and power lines were wrecked.

In 1978, Vietnam entered into another war, this time with Cambodia. In 1975, a brutal communist group called the Khmer Rouge had taken power there. The Khmer Rouge launched repeated raids on Vietnam. With the support of the Soviet Union, Vietnam invaded Cambodia and replaced the Khmer Rouge with a new

HOW THE GOVERNMENT WORKS

Vietnam is a socialist state governed by the Communist Party of Vietnam. Everyone over the age of 18 can vote. The National Assembly, with 498 members, is the highest law-making body. About 90 percent of its members belong to the Communist Party. The National Assembly is led by a chairman. The prime minister runs the government and appoints ministers. The president is head of state and commander of the armed forces. Another powerful force in Vietnam is the Communist Party's 14-strong Politburo. Its members are elected by the party. The Politburo nominates many public officials and decides on government policies. The National Assembly and government then turn those policies into law.

PRESIDENT		
EXECUTIVE	LEGISLATIVE	JUDICIARY
PRIME MINISTER	CHAIRMAN	SUPREME COURT
CABINET	NATIONAL ASSEMBLY (498 MEMBERS)	PROVINCIAL COURTS

government. In response, China, an ally of the Khmer Rouge, attacked Vietnam's northern border. Vietnam's troops drove the Chinese back, but also had to fight the Khmer Rouge in Cambodia. The war dragged on until 1989.

Many Changes

At home, the government began the task of rebuilding the country. The state took control of factories and organized farms into cooperatives. People were not allowed to run their own businesses, and there was very little money coming from abroad. The United States imposed a trade ban, called an embargo, on Vietnam. Vietnam traded with other communist nations, but it did not make enough money to spend on developing the country.

In 1986, the Vietnamese government announced a more open economic policy, called *doi-moi*. Small private businesses were encouraged; land was divided up into more family farms, and the state gave up control of many industries. The aim was to encourage foreign companies to spend money in Vietnam.

Almost overnight, small businesses such as shops and workshops sprang up all over the country. Asian nations including Singapore, Taiwan, and Japan began to build factories in Vietnam, and the economy

▲ In the Central Highlands, an elephant is used to transport construction material.

▼ A veteran of the war in Cambodia shows off his artificial legs. His own legs were blown off by a landmine. Millions of mines still remain buried in Cambodia.

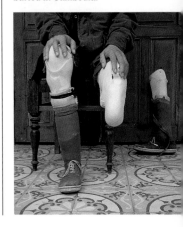

PROPAGANDA ART

▲ Cyclists pass a poster that encourages members of Vietnamese society to work harder.

Art has played a role in Vietnamese politics since the 1940s when many artists expressed the people's desire for independence from France. Since 1954, the communist government has spread its message using propaganda posters. There are about ten full-time propaganda artists, but many more are employed to produce images occasionally. The pictures are a record of changes taking place within Vietnam as the country industrializes rapidly. Recent posters show office workers and computer programmers, as well as the soldiers, engineers, and farmers who dominated the art form a few decades ago.

▼ Ducks are bundled up for sale. About 10,000 live ducks are sold in this Ho Chi Minh City market each day.

developed quickly. The collapse of many of Vietnam's communist former trading partners in the late 1980s did not damage economic development. In 1994, Vietnam joined the Association of Southeast Asian Nations, which organizes trade in the region. In the same year, the United States lifted its embargo and resumed trade relations with Vietnam. The two countries eventually signed a formal trade agreement in 2001.

Land and Sea

Half of all Vietnam's workers are farmers or fishers. Agriculture and fishing together earn one-fifth of the country's money. However, this share of the total is likely to go down as other parts of the economy grow. Rice is the main crop—Vietnam is the world's third-largest rice exporter. The country produces several other crops for sale abroad, including coffee, tea, and rubber. Farmers also raise chickens, ducks, pigs, and cattle—mainly for meat and eggs, because Vietnamese people do not like to drink milk, or eat cheese and other dairy products.

Vietnam's wetlands yield huge catches of fish and shellfish. Shrimp farming is a large industry in coastal areas. However, stretches of wild mangrove forest are being destroyed to create space for shrimp farms.

Working Hard

A third of Vietnamese workers are involved in manufacturing and mining, which amounts to 42 percent of the economy. Clothing and textiles, including silk, are the most

▲ Rice is measured out into sacks at a rice market beside the Red River.

▼ A fisher makes last-minute repairs to a giant net before it is lowered into the sea.

Women sew clothes to be sold in shops around the world.

▼ Factory reels contain fibers of silk that have been carefully unraveled from the cocoons of silk moths. Factories like this one have made fine silk clothes much less expensive to produce.

important products. Vietnam also manufactures fertilizer, glass, steel, and tires. Electronic equipment such as TVs and refrigerators are produced mainly for sale at home.

Vietnam is rich in minerals, including iron ore, tin, zinc, chromite, copper, gold, and lead. Bauxite is used to make aluminium, silica to make glass, and phosphate is used in fertilizer. Limestone is mined for cement. Large coal fields lie in the north. Oil and gas are found in coastal waters. Crude oil is one of Vietnam's most valuable exports.

Paid to Serve

Service industries are types of work that sell services rather than manufactured goods or farm produce.

About a quarter of Vietnam's workers are employed in service industries, but they make up 38 percent of the economy. Service industries include transportation, banking, government, education, health, and tourism.

Tourism has grown rapidly in the last 20

NATION OF TWO WHEELS

The traditional forms of transportation in Vietnam are bicycles and tricycle-rickshaws, known as cyclos. However as people become richer, they are turning to motorized transport—motorcycles and scooters. City streets now throb to the roar of engines. More than 14,000 people apply for driving licenses each month in Hanoi alone, and authorities suspect that is only half the real number of new drivers. The government encourages people to wear helmets, but many Vietnamese do not.

▲ A family of four rides on one motorcycle.

years. In 1992, 400,000 foreign tourists came to Vietnam. That number rose to 1.7 million in 1997, then 3.6 million in 2006. Tourism has increased the need for people to work as taxi drivers, tour guides, waiters, and hotel staff in Vietnam.

Toward the Future

Vietnam's economy has made great strides since the late 1980s. In 1997, the economy continued to grow despite a recession (slump in economic activity) in the rest of Southeast Asia. In 2001, the government announced a new aim to transform Vietnam into an industrialized nation by 2020.

In 2006, a new president was elected. Nguyen Minh Triet is a modernizer. He says he will cut

INDUSTRY MAP

Vietnam's mineral reserves include coal, iron ore, and bauxite from the northern mountains. Extensive oil and gas fields lie off the coast. The south is the main industrial zone. Ho Chi Minh City is known for its electronics industry. However, factories are poorly regulated and release pollution which harms the environment.

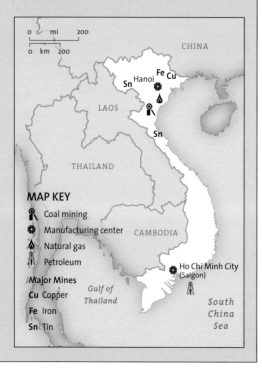

CHINA

o mi 200

o km 200

Sn Hanoi Fe Cu

LAOS

Sn

THAILAND

MAP KEY

Coal mining

Manufacturing center   CAMBODIA

Natural gas

Petroleum

Major Mines

Cu Copper   Gulf of
             Thailand

Fe Iron

Sn Tin

Ho Chi Minh City
(Saigon)

South
China
Sea

government control over people and businesses in order to make it easier for people to make money. In 2007, Vietnam joined the World Trade Organization, which will help reduce barriers on imports to Vietnam and Vietnamese exports overseas.

Rich and Poor

Cities such as Ho Chi Minh City contain growing numbers of prosperous middle-class people. These are successful businesspeople who live in comfortable homes and can afford luxury goods such as cars and large TVs.

However, Vietnam is still a very poor country by world standards. Many people earn less than one dollar a day. Many farm workers have moved to urban areas to find jobs. Economic progress has improved the standard of living for virtually all parts of society, but there is a growing divide between a small number of rich people and the rest of the population. During the economic reforms of the 1980s, the government could no longer spend so much on health, education, and other public services. Recently, however, spending on education has risen rapidly.

Big Challenges

Vietnam's government faces a tough challenge: to make the country rich without losing the benefits and fairness of communism, such as high standards of education and healthcare. As the country becomes increasingly industrial, environmental protection must also become a priority. Vietnam's forests are being raided for their lumber, and animals are losing their natural habitats.

▲ Tourists are greeted as their ship arrives in Ho Chi Minh City's harbor.

On the positive side, the government can count on the determination and optimism of its people. All over Vietnam, people see that things are slowly getting better. While not forgetting their past, the Vietnamese are looking to the future as they work to rebuild their country and improve their lives.

▼ Modern office and apartment buildings rise above Hanoi.

Add a Little Extra to Your Country Report!

If you are assigned to write a report about Vietnam, you'll want to include basic information about the country, of course. The Fast Facts chart on page 8 will give you a good start. The rest of the book will give you the details you need to create a full and up-to-date paper or PowerPoint presentation. But what can you do to make your report more fun than anyone else's? If you use your imagination and dig a bit deeper into some of the topics introduced in this book, you're sure to come up with information that will make your report unique!

>Flag

Perhaps you could explain the history of Vietnam's flag, and the meanings of its colors and symbol. Go to **www.crwflags.com/fotw/flags** for more information.

>National Anthem

How about downloading Vietnam's national anthem, and playing it for your class? At **www.nationalanthems.info** you'll find what you need, including the words to the anthem, plus sheet music for it. Simply pick "V" and then "Vietnam" from the list on the left-hand side of the screen, and you're on your way.

>Time Difference

If you want to understand the time difference between Vietnam and where you are, this Web site can help: **www.worldtimeserver.com**. Just pick "Vietnam" from the list on the left. If you called someone in Vietnam right now, would you wake them up from their sleep?

>Currency

Another Web site will
convert your money into
dong, the currency
used in Vietnam.
You'll want to know
how much money to
bring if you're ever
lucky enough to
travel to Vietnam:
www.xe.com/ucc.

>Weather

Why not check the current weather in Vietnam? It's easy—go to
www.weather.com to find out if it's sunny or cloudy, warm or cold in
Vietnam right now! Pick "World" from the headings at the top of the
page. Then search for the Vietnam. Click on any city. Be sure to click on
the tabs below the weather report for Sunrise/Sunset information,
Weather Watch, and Business Travel Outlook, too. Scroll down the page
for the 36-hour Forecast and a satellite weather map. Compare your
weather to the weather in the Vietnamese city you chose. Is this a good
season, weather-wise, for a person to travel to Vietnam?

>Miscellaneous

Still want more information? Simply go to National Geographic's World
Atlas for Young Explorers site at **http://www.nationalgeographic.com/
kids-world-atlas/**. It will help you find maps, photos, music, games, and
other features that you can use to jazz up your report.

Glossary

Antelope a type of hoofed animal with horns that is related to cattle, sheep, and goats. Antelopes live in Africa and Asia only. They include wildebeests, waterbucks, and oryxs.

Citadel a fortress built to command a city, often located on a hill or another high point.

Climate the average weather of a certain place at different times of year.

Colony a region that is ruled by a nation located somewhere else in the world. Settlers from that distant country take the land from the region's original inhabitants.

Communist a system of government where a single political party rules a country with the job of ensuring that wealth is shared equally among all the people in the country.

Cooperative a business that is jointly owned by several families. Vietnam used to have many cooperative farms.

Culture a collection of beliefs, traditions, and styles that belongs to people living in a certain part of the world.

Delta the mouth of a river where the stream splits into two or more branches. The split streams form a triangle shape called a delta for the Greek letter .

Economy the system by which a country creates wealth through making and trading in products.

Ecosystem a community of living things and the environment they interact with; an ecosystem includes plants, animals, soil, water, and air.

Habitat a part of the environment that is suitable for certain plants and animals.

Irrigation taking water from a river or a well to use on fields and in plantations.

Nomadic when a person does not have a fixed home and instead moves regularly from place to place in order to find food.

Peninsula a narrow piece of land that is surrounded by water on three sides. The word means "almost island" in Latin.

Petroleum oil and gas that is pumped up from beneath the surface of the Earth. Petroleum is refined to make gasoline and other fuels and provides the raw materials for plastics.

Policy a plan adopted by a government to address a particular problem. A policy might require a new law being made.

Propaganda information produced by a government. Sometimes certain facts are altered to make the government look good.

Silt very fine soil and clay that is carried by large rivers. As it settles to the riverbed, silt forms deep mud.

Species a type of organism; animals or plants in the same species look similar and can only breed successfully among themselves.

Stalactite a pointed structure that hangs from the roof of a cave or overhanging rock. Stalactites are formed over many thousands of years as droplets of salty water leave tiny layers of crystals on the rock.

Stalagmite a pointed structure that rises up from the ground, normally inside a cave. Stalagmites form in a similar process to stalactites, but from water dripping onto the ground. Stalagmites often form under stalactites and eventually the two join to form a column.

Bibliography

Imbriaco, Alison. *Vietnam.* Berkeley Heights, NJ: MyReportLinks.com, 2004.

Ng, Yumi. *Welcome to Vietnam.* Milwaukee, WI: Gareth Stevens Pub., 2003.

Taus-Bolstad, Stacy. *Vietnam in Pictures.* Minneapolis, MN: Lerner Publications, 2003.

http://www.cpv.org.vn/index_e.html (official Web site of the Communist Party of Vietnam)

http://lcweb2.loc.gov/frd/cs/vntoc.html (general information)

http://news.bbc.co.uk/1/hi/world/asia-pacific/country_profiles/1243338.stm (general information)

Further Information

NATIONAL GEOGRAPHIC Articles

Lamb, David. "Hanoi: Shedding the Ghosts of War." NATIONAL GEOGRAPHIC (May 2004): 80–97.

Rendon, Joni. "Ho Chi Minh City." NATIONAL GEOGRAPHIC TRAVELER (July/August 2006): 108.

Web sites to explore

More fast facts about Vietnam, from the CIA (Central Intelligence Agency): https://www.cia.gov/library/publications/the-world-factbook/geos/vm.html

At the height of the Vietnam War in 1969, more than half a million U.S. soldiers were fighting in the country. Find out more about what it was like for them at this PBS site: http://www.pbs.org/battlefieldvietnam/

Take a journey through the paddies, towns, and forests of the Mekong Delta by looking at the great photographs on this site: http://www.vietscape.com/travel/mekong/

Ho Chi Minh, or Uncle Ho as he is known by most Vietnamese, was the most important figure in the country's recent history. Read about his life here: www.time.com/time/time100/leaders/profile/hochiminh.html

Vietnam has rich musical traditions. Listen to some of the instruments used and see how they are played at this Web site: http://www.geocities.com/saigonstrings/sounds.htm

Take a look at the work of some of Vietnam's greatest living artists at this site: http://www.vietnamartist.com/

See, hear

There are many ways to get a taste of life in Vietnam, such as movies, music, magazines, or TV shows. You might be able to locate these:

Voice of Vietnam
Find out what is happening in Vietnam by reading the news on the Web site of Vietnam's international radio service, VOV: http://www.vov.org.vn/

Boat People (1993)
This novel by Mary Gardner tells the story of Vietnamese Americans living in Galveston, Texas, where they have settled after fleeing southern Vietnam when the communists took power.

Index

Credits

Picture Credits

NGIC = National Geographic Image Collection

Front Cover – Spine: Justin Guariglia/NGIC; Top: H. Justin Guariglia/NGIC; Low Far Left: Steve Raymer/NGIC; Low Left: Steve Raymer/NGIC; Low Right: David Alan Harvey/NGIC; Low Far Right: Paul Chesley/NGIC.

Interior – Corbis: Bettmann: 29 lo; Bohemian Nomad Picturemakers: 52 up; Dan Bool/Sygma: 57 lo; Tom BRakefield: 18 lo; W. Perry Conway: 2 right, 14-15; Alain Dejean/Sygma: 33 up; Free Agents Limited: 43 lo; Catherine Karnow: 30 up; Jacques Pavlovsky/Sygma: 33 lo; Steve Raymer: 2 left, 6-7, 45 lo; Reuters 13 up; Julian Abram Wainwright/epa: 42 up; Terry Whittaker/FLPA: 16 lo; NGIC: Paul Chesley: 5 up, 13 lo; W. E. Gerrett 31 up; Justin Guariglia: 29 up; David Alan Harvey: 32 lo, 39 up; Karen Kasmauski: 3 left, 34-35, 52 lo; Tim Laman: 21 center; Frans Lanting: 20 up; Michael Lewis: 11 up; Gina Martin: 42 lo; Stephanie Maze: TP, 40 center, 45 up, 54 lo; Winfield Parks: 27 up; Steve Raymer: 2-3, 3 right, 10 up, 11 lo, 12 lo, 18 up, 22-23, 24 up, 26 up, 28 center, 31 lo, 36 lo, 38 center, 39 lo, 41 up, 41 lo, 44 up, 46-47, 51 up, 53 up, 53 lo, 54 up, 56 up, 57 up; Hope Ryden: 19 up; Maggie Steber: 51 lo; Peter M. Wilson 27 lo; Michael S. Yamashita: 20 lo, 48 lo; Photos.com: 59 up.

Text copyright © 2008 National Geographic Society
Published by the National Geographic Society.

For more information, please call 1-800-NGS-LINE (647-5463) or write to the following address:

NATIONAL GEOGRAPHIC SOCIETY
1145 17th Street N.W.
Washington, D.C. 20036-4688 U.S.A.

Visit the Society's Web site at
www.nationalgeographic.com/books

Library of Congress Cataloging-in-Publication Data available on request
ISBN: 978-1-4263-0202-2

Printed in the United States of America

Series design by Jim Hiscott.
The body text is set in Avenir; Knockout.
The display text is set in Matrix Script.

Front Cover—Top: A vegetable seller passes a store in Hanoi; Low Far Left: Musicians in traditional costume at the Palace of Supreme Harmony, Hue; Low Left: Rice fields near Lao Cai; Low Right: A woman touches the feet of a statue of Buddha, Hanoi; Low Far Right: Motorbikes during New Year celebrations.

Page 1—Schoolchildren line up before class; Icon image on spine, Contents page, and throughout: Conical straw hats, Hoi An

Produced through the worldwide resources of the National Geographic Society

John M. Fahey, Jr., *President and Chief Executive Officer*; Gilbert M. Grosvenor, *Chairman of the Board*; Nina D. Hoffman, *Executive Vice President, President of Book Publishing Group*

National Geographic Staff for this Book

Nancy Laties Feresten, *Vice President, Editor-in-Chief of Children's Books*
Bea Jackson, *Director of Design and Illustration*
Jim Hiscott, *Art Director*
Priyanka Lamichhane, *Project Editor*
Lori Epstein, *Illustrations Editor*
Stacy Gold, Nadia Hughes, *Illustrations Research Editors*
R. Gary Colbert, *Production Director*
Lewis R. Bassford, *Production Manager*
Maryclare Tracy, Nicole Elliott, *Manufacturing Managers*
Maps, *Mapping Specialists, Ltd.*

Brown Reference Group plc. Staff for this Book

Volume Editor: Tom Jackson
Designer: Dave Allen
Picture Manager: Clare Newman
Maps: Martin Darlison
Artwork: Darren Awuah
Index: Kay Ollerenshaw
Senior Managing Editor: Tim Cooke
Design Manager: Sarah Williams
Children's Publisher: Anne O'Daly
Editorial Director: Lindsey Lowe

About the Author

JEN GREEN received a doctorate from the University of Sussex, United Kingdom, in 1982. She worked in publishing for 15 years and is now a full-time author who has written more than 150 books for children on natural history, geography, history, the environment, and other subjects.

About the Consultants

PETER ZINOMAN is associate professor of History and Southeast Asian Studies at the University of California, Berkeley. His research focuses on the modern history and literature of Vietnam. His book *The Colonial Bastille: A History of Imprisonment in Vietnam, 1862-1940* (2001) won the Harry Benda Prize from the Association of Asian Studies and the John Fairbank Prize from the American Historical Association. He is the founding editor-in-chief of the *Journal of Vietnamese Studies.*

HY V. LUONG is Professor of Anthropology at the University of Toronto, Canada. He has published extensively on discourse, gender, social structure, political economy, and sociocultural transformation in contemporary Vietnam. He has regularly conducted comparative field research in northern and southern Vietnam since 1987.

Time Line of
Vietnamese History

B.C.

ca 800 The Dong Son culture of northern Vietnam develops bronze-working.

207 Trieu Da forms Nam Viet, independent of Chinese control.

111 The Chinese Han dynasty incorporates Nam Viet into their empire.

A.D.

ca 100 The state of Funan emerges around the Mekong Delta; the Cham kingdom of Lam Ap is formed in central Vietnam.

541 Ly Bi leads a six-year revolt against Chinese rule in Vietnam.

618–907 The Chinese Tang dynasty strengthens its control of northern Vietnam.

939 Ngo Quyen defeats Chinese forces at the Battle of Bach Dang, officially marking an end to a thousand years of Chinese control of northern Vietnam.

968 Dinh Bo Linh founds an independent kingdom in northern Vietnam.

1010 The Ly dynasty is established; in 1054 it renames the country Dai Viet.

1400

1407 China conquers Vietnam.

1428 General Le Loi forces the Chinese out of Dai Viet and expands Dai Viet into Champa territory.

1600

1626 Civil war begins in Vietnam; the war lasts forty-seven years.

1651 Alexandre de Rhodes, a French Jesuit monk, publishes a dictionary that uses quoc ngu, a system that writes the Vietnamese language in the Roman alphabet.

1800

1802 Nguyen Anh defeats the Tay Son rebellion and unifies Vietnam, with Hue as the capital.

1856 French forces, eager to spread their influence, attack the city of Da Nang.

1862 France takes control of half of Cochinchina, the southern part of Vietnam.

1867 French forces establish control over all of Cochinchina.

1887 France establishes the Indochinese Union, which includes Vietnam and Cambodia and, later, Laos.

1900

1930 Ho Chi Minh founds the Indochinese Communist Party.

1940 Japan occupies Vietnam but leaves the French administration in place during World War II.

1941 The Indochinese Communist Party organizes the Viet Minh, a guerrilla force that resists Japanese occupation.

1945 The Viet Minh takes control of Vietnam from the Japanese and Ho Chi Minh announces the country's independence.

1946 The Indochinese War begins when French troops attack the Viet Minh in Haiphong.